God's Nobody

By

Joshua M. Coverett

Acknowledgment

I am extremely thankful for my wife Amy. She is the one that encouraged me to write this book. We both have a sincere love for teenagers and desire to help them see how important they are to God. A few years back, Amy asked me if I would consider writing a book. She told me that there are many teens going through the same feelings I went through as a teenager. She stressed the importance of helping them understand how God is preparing them for great things.

Through the years Amy has stood by my side. She has made many sacrifices, and continues to support me in the ministry we have together. Her love for God is evident through her love for others. Thank you, Amy, for the time you have sacrificed and the love you have shown to me, to God, and to the teenagers that read this book. We are all grateful for your love.

I would also like to thank the members of Calvary Independent Baptist Church for supporting me in the publishing of this book. May God bless each and every one of you for your willingness to reach out to "the uttermost part of the earth".

Dedication

This book is dedicated to the teens. If you are a teenager, this one's for you. I believe teenagers have more potential than they will ever realize. God continually used teenagers throughout the Bible. Why? — Because they had what it took to get the job done. They still have what it takes. There is a special quality all teenagers possess. They are beginning to search for purpose, and now is the best time to find it.

Teenager, I believe in you and so does God. You do have what it takes to impact this world for Christ. God has His eye on you. You are so important to Him. Keep pressing on. God has great things in store for you.

Table of Contents

God's Nobody 11

Let's Talk, Nobody to Nobody 21

The Day God Gave Us Control 43

Doctor We Have No "Patience" 59

Roaches and Holiness 71

Puppy Love is True Love 83

Identity Crisis 97

It's Not My Life; It's My Turn. 107

Have You Totally Lost It 121

Go For It! 127

About the Author 129

God's Nobody

It was amazing! The crowd was in awe. What just happened was unbelievable. This young teenager had just picked up a spare in bowling. It was not even an easy spare to pick up. He had just knocked over the last few pins of the game. There was something extra special about these pins though. These were record-breaking pins. These pins would mean a new high score. After the pins fell, the young man turned to face the crowd. They could hardly believe what they had just seen. This teenager had just done the impossible. It was incredible. Some of the people were laughing. Others had scowls on their faces. How in the world did he do it?

To pick up a record-breaking spare would normally have been a good thing. This, however, was not good at all. Under any other circumstances this would have been a proud moment for the boy, but this time he was humiliated. He had just thrown the ball down the lane and into the gutter. The ball just happened to have enough spin on it to bounce back out. It bounced the wrong way though. The teenager watched in horror as his ball jumped over into the lane of the bowling league next to him. These were skilled bowlers. He had just knocked over the record-breaking pins of the man bowling next to him. As he turned around, his family and friends were laughing and the members of the bowling league were standing in shock. How could this happen?

This is a true story. Believe me — I know. I was the teenager. I have never been able to forget the events of that day. I was humiliated. Up to that point in my life it was the most embarrassing thing I had ever done. I wanted to crawl under the bowling alley to escape from the laughter. I felt like a misfit. I felt like a "nobody".

I'm sure this exact thing has never happened to you, but you can probably relate to it. Maybe you made a touch-down for the opposing team. You may have fallen off a stage or walked into a wall. We have all experienced something we would go back and erase if we could. Do you remember the way you felt? It was embarrassing. You felt like a loser. You were a "nobody." The longer this kind of thing goes on, the worse you feel. After awhile you feel like you have no purpose. I was a happy teenager. I loved to make people laugh and I enjoyed life most of the time. I really did have a good life, but that question that had previously entered my mind continued to bother me. What is my purpose in life?

Have you ever wondered why you are here? Why did God place you on this earth? Does He have a purpose for your life? If so, what is it? There has to be a plan. God doesn't just do things without having some reason. So where do you fit in this plan? What is your purpose? These are questions that every teenager has asked themselves. There must be an answer to why we exist. Everyone wants to be needed. We all want to know what our purpose in life is.

As you read this book you will find the answers to these questions. You will also get to hear several stories like the one about my bowling experience. That's right, now I have your attention. It is kind of funny how that works. You see, it never makes your day when you walk into a door while eating an ice cream cone, as a crowd of people stare straight at you. But, when you see someone else do it, it's totally hilarious.

Many Hollywood producers rely on this fact. They know their movies will get a laugh if the characters in it are going through a succession of bad luck. People find this stuff to be funny. For example — if an open bucket of paint were to fall upside-down on your head, suddenly, you would be having a bad day. If the bucket of paint fell on your friend's head however, you have found a reason to smile and instantly your day has become better. God has given us all the ability to find somebody else's bad luck a little bit humorous. So, don't put the book down yet. You may be missing something that you really needed to read about. It may even help you through some tough times in your own life, but if nothing else, you had a good laugh.

Although this book was not written just to make you smile, I hope it does. What I really want you to know is that someone out there does understand what it is like to be a teenager. I know it is not easy. There is a common problem many adults have that causes them to be distanced from the up-and-coming generation of teenagers. I have heard many parents say, "I don't understand where I went wrong. What do they want? Why do they act the way they do?" Now we have what we call a "generation gap."

This gap is not like a little tiny crack in the sidewalk. No, this gap is more like the Grand Canyon. Trying to get across it without a bridge of understanding is basically suicide. I hope that by reading this book you can start building that bridge. I cannot even begin to tell you how many times parents have asked me why their sons and daughters behave the way they do. Of course, they wanted me to tell them right away so that the whole world would be a better place to live, but I had to ask the one person that would know best — the teenager. Do you think everything went smooth when I approached that teenager and said, "Go ahead, tell me why you do the things you do? Tell me why you feel the way you do?" No. Sure, it would have been great if the teenager would have said, "Let me tell you all about it." Did they do that? Nope — they didn't know either.

Here are a series of questions I have asked teenagers in the past. Do you know who you really are? Why do you do the things you do? Why are you here? What do you want out of life? Does God have big plans for you? Do you feel important or special in any way?

Here are the series of answers I got back from them. "I don't know." That's right. They don't know. If you have ever been in a situation that was similar to this, you understand where they were coming from. Not knowing why you even exist is extremely troubling, but not knowing who you are is even worse. Now you are a "nobody" sitting on this planet with no specific purpose in mind. Sounds fun, huh? Chances are you know exactly what I am talking about. You may even be going through it right now. I do understand — I was there.

Before we go any farther I want you to realize where I am. I am no longer living in that hopeless "state of confusion," wondering who I am or why I even exist. I do not consider that my home anymore. I got out! Now, I am writing to you from the other side, but I have never forgotten what it was like. While I was there, all I wanted was to find a way out. I just wanted to know who I was and why God put me here.

By the end of this book, I believe you will find the answers to this problem. I think you will enjoy hearing about all the things that God allowed me to go through when I was a teenager. You may even be able to sympathize with me.

There have been many times when I thought God had forgotten about me, or that maybe I was just the punch line to some really bad joke. I know these thoughts have probably crossed your mind before too. God hasn't forgotten about you. He loves you very much. You are here for a purpose. God has plans for you. If He did not want you here, you would not be here. Believe me, God needs you. Sometimes He just has a funny way of molding us into what He wants us to be. Looking back on my life I realize that it can be a really funny way. He was able to use the circumstances in my life to show me the purpose He had for me. Now I am proud to say that I know my purpose. I am "God's Nobody".

Ask Yourself This

— What am I searching for in life? _____

_____

— Who do I want to become? _____

_____

— Do I sincerely want to know God's purpose
for my life? _____

— Am I ready to <u>truly</u> seek His will?

_____

Memorize This:

**John 3:30 "He must increase,
but I must decrease."**

Let's Talk
(Nobody to Nobody)

Oh, this is great. The author himself thinks he's a "nobody". How in the world can this book help me get past these feelings of confusion when the author believes he is a "nobody"? Hold on there partner. I have a feeling that hearing this from a "nobody" will help more than if you heard it from a "somebody". I have found that when I have a problem in life, it is best to go to someone who understands. In no way do I want you to think I am calling myself a loser. I am just a "nobody". I am also not just any "nobody" — I am God's "nobody".

The title "Nobody" and the title "God's Nobody" have two totally different definitions. They are complete opposites. I remember what it was like to feel that I had no specific purpose in life or that I just didn't know who I was. That is why I think this book can really help.

I don't know of too many people who would go to a professional hockey player to get their dental work done. We all want to go to someone who knows something about our specific needs. Someone who knows what they are talking about or has experience in your area of need can be of much more help than someone who really doesn't understand. I remember being a teenager. It is one of those memories that will be burned into my head for eternity. Most adults try to forget about their teenage years, and I think we all know why. They can be rough, but they can also be just the thing that reveals who you really are.

The great thing about not knowing who you are is that it is not a life-long thing. When we are children we have no concern about who we are or what we will be. The only thing that is on our mind is what to get into next. We are carefree. We enjoy chasing each other in imaginary cars, picking flowers, and getting muddy. We didn't need to know who we were going to be. Who we were was enough.

Then one day it happened. Whether it was a sibling that hit us over the head while we were sleeping or a meteor that crashed into us; we may never know. The one thing we do know is that we had a serious case of identity-amnesia take over us. We forgot who we were. One day we were carefree and the next day we were confused. It is really not that important to find out how it happened. We just want to know who we are.

I can almost pinpoint the day my amnesia attacked. I was sitting in my room playing with my

Legos. Suddenly I was surrounded by this mature voice that was calling me a baby. No one was in the room with me. I was playing with my toys all by myself. Once I realized it was just my imagination, I began to play again. Then my game started to get really intense.

Legos were flying everywhere. Lego men were pulling each other's arms and legs off and re-attaching them to buildings and vehicles. A war had begun in my Lego world and it had to be stopped. It was time to send in reinforcements.

G.I. Joes and Hot Wheel cars were called to the scene and the prayers of the stuffed animals were with every soldier on the field. The battle was raging. Towns were being destroyed and it was all because of a Hershey's Kiss that was trapped behind enemy lines.

The chaos was overwhelming and the cries of the stuffed animals were heard throughout the land. Something had to be done. This battle had to stop. One lone Hot Wheel had the answer. It was risky, but it needed to be done. He realized that he alone could stop this war if he would heroically leap from the bed and crash through the building where the Kiss was being held hostage.

The tension and suspense was growing greater as he approached the edge of the bed. As he flew through the air and into the building, I made the crashing sound effects with my voice to add to the excitement. Right then, I heard that voice again saying, "You baby". Then I started thinking that I was a thirteen year old man playing with toys.

Was I a child or was I a man? Was it okay for me to play with toys or should I grow up? Was I being immature or was this behavior acceptable? Who was I? I was lost and confused. I really didn't know who I was or how I was supposed to act. My amnesia had set in, and I was lost. That day was the beginning of a really rotten friendship with myself. I started changing. I was growing to dislike myself and I was taking it out on others.

My two brothers and my sister were starting to see me change from day to day. I was not happy and I didn't know how to be happy. It's amazing how it works when a person is unhappy. They either start to throw a pity party or they force everyone they come in contact with into their unhappiness. My little brother was my choice victim. If I was unhappy, then he must be unhappy too.

My brother was a typical little brother. He wanted to hang out with me and mimic my every move. This used to be cool to me. We would sit down and play Legos together and try to solve the world's problems. We were a team. But all of that was about to change.

Remember, I was confused. I didn't know where I belonged. Now, when my brother would come up to me and ask me to play, I would look at him as if I were surprised at his behavior. Asking a mature adult, like myself, to play a childish game of Legos was ridiculous. What was he thinking? Inside I wanted to play more than anything. Outside I showed no interest. I was fighting against myself and I didn't know which side to cheer for.

I was starting to treat anyone younger than me like a child. I was also trying to fit in with the adult crowd. I would push my friends away and try to be more mature. I would watch my friends do the things I knew were fun to do, but I couldn't associate myself with that anymore. I was a man now!

Gradually I was becoming bored with my existence, so I started going back to who I was before. It is a good thing that my brothers and sister got bored from time to time, or I may have never been allowed back into that bond we had. I messed up, but they forgave me. I was back! The cool big brother had entered the building. I was able to be a kid again and I was happy. We would sword fight with paper towel rolls and run in circles until we were too dizzy to stand up. We laughed about stupid things and watched cartoons together. That was the life. I was free and happy again.

I felt alive and on top of the world. My siblings thought I was cool and they wanted to hang out with me. We talked and played together all of the time. They were my friends. Then I heard the Boogie Man again. You see, it was not uncommon for me to hang out with my siblings all day every day. That is just the way we did things. It was my life. Then "she" came along.

There was a girl who lived several blocks away from me, that didn't even know I existed. This girl had grabbed a hold of my attention and was holding on tight. I knew what had to be done. I knew what my purpose was – at least for that moment. I was to make the biggest fool of myself while truly believing that I was winning over the heart of this fair maiden. I would walk into her life and she would fall madly in love with me. At least that was my plan.

God had a different idea though. In order for my idea to work I needed to leave my siblings behind again. I needed to show this girl that I was ready to be a man. All my childish days were behind me. It just turned out that this approach of mine would work out great for God's plan too. It had to be done.

I had to show this girl, whom I really didn't know at all, that I was the man she had been dreaming of all her life. It was time to go into plan "A". Remember, at the time I was insecure about who I was. My self-esteem was not very high at all. These are not good qualities to have when you are about to steal the heart of a young lady.

For God, these were just the qualities I needed. It was almost as if I were struck by lightning. One moment I was insecure, and the next moment I had more courage and confidence than ever before. Plan "A" had begun. I saw her walking down the street along with a friend. Did this friend make me hesitate? No. This would make an even greater impression. Being a man who could show his feelings even when others were around would be just the thing to win her over to me.

With every step I lost a little courage, but I kept walking. Then we were face to face, and it was time for me to say the words that would melt her heart and make her mine forever. I had to choose them wisely. These words were going to ring in her ears for years to come. We would both look back one day and hear those words that brought us together.

Before I knew it, they started pouring out of my mouth as if I had a verbal leak. I did it. I had said the words that secured me a spot in the list of people with the worst pick up lines of all time. "You're kind of cute". Yep, that's what I said. I was the leader of all village idiots. After those four words so gracefully stumbled out of my mouth, the leak was repaired. I could no longer speak. She had the same problem. She couldn't speak either, because her laughter was getting in the way. That is when I switched to Plan "B". I would go back home and speak of this to no one. As a matter of fact, you are the first that I have ever mentioned it to.

Did God not see what was happening to me? Couldn't He have stopped me from going through this embarrassing moment as a teenager? I guess He could have if He had wanted to, but He didn't want to. God wanted to teach me something that day, and He got His point across very effectively. I did not need to grow up at the speed that I was trying to. I needed to be humble. I needed to look at those around me and focus on them rather than on myself. When I was trying to be the manly teenager that I wasn't, I was scaring people away. No one wanted to be around me. When I showed an interest in who others were, they desired to be near me. A girlfriend wasn't what I needed at the time. Humility was what I needed. God saw my need and used my inexperience to supply it for me.

— — — — — **No, Body, No!** — — — — —-

Like most people, I had to learn my lesson the hard way. This one event was not going to do the trick. God had to remind me again. My own body is what He decided to use as His tool. I needed to learn how to be humble. I did not need a humbling experience. I needed a life change.

If we want to grow in maturity and wisdom, we must first learn to be humble. James 4:10 says, *"Humble yourselves in the sight of the Lord, and he shall lift you up"*. It is not something we need to do ourselves. He will lift us up. We do not need to try to figure out what our specific purpose in life is. He knows what we are here for and He will reveal it to us when it is time. First, He needs to get us to that place where He can use us. I was about to learn that lesson also.

I was fourteen years old when my body started betraying me. God was still in control and my body was out of control. My first pimple was born. It had come out to see what the world was like. It saw that the air was clear and that life was worth experiencing, so it went back to get all of its friends and family.

Before I knew it, I was hosting the pimple party of the year. Every pimple and its brother showed up for the celebration. No invitations were needed. If you were a pimple, this was the place to be. Well, I did not appreciate these pimples going around my authority. They were throwing this party without my permission, so I took matters into my own hands. I decided to throw an acne remedy party.

I started using anything on the market to break up the pimple party. All that did was make the pimples mad. They did not leave. They brought in reinforcements. I was not able to control my own face. The hunk of a man that I was supposed to be, in my own mind, had turned into a pimple plantation. This was just the beginning of my body taking over.

Have you ever heard someone who was trying to learn a new instrument? It sounds horrible. Well, inside my voice box some kind-hearted individual was trying to teach my vocal cords several new instruments at one time. Sure, my voice was not very manly before, but this was ridiculous. Every time I tried to say something that sounded half way intelligent, my voice would crack. It sounded as if I was trying to yodel everything I said. I thought God had turned His back for just a second, and boy, was He going to be surprised when He turned back around. I was out of control. I had turned into a yodeling pimple and I was not pleased.

Teenagers have a reputation to maintain. Their peers expect them to be cool. I had fallen short of all of their expectations. My self-esteem was low and I thought everybody looked at me funny. There were many days that I went to my room to be alone. I didn't want anyone to see me because I didn't like looking at myself. I was depressed and embarrassed because of what I was becoming.

Maybe you know exactly what I am talking about. Maybe you have felt that same way from time to time. Don't give up. It does get better. I promise. God never makes mistakes. He made you just the way you are, and what makes that awesome is the fact that He did not make you from a mold. He made you for a special purpose that only you can fulfill. You are the only one who can do what God has made you for. He needs you.

That is a sobering thought isn't it? God needs you. An almighty, all-knowing, all-powerful God needs you. I remember the first time I heard those words. I was sitting at camp listening to the speaker give a message to a group of teenagers who thought they were losers. I really thought I was a loser too. When the speaker looked into the audience it seemed as if he was looking straight at me. He said those words, "God needs you". I thought the same thing that most teenagers think when they hear that – for what? I had no talents. I couldn't sing, speak, or even walk straight half of the time. What could He use me for? I was getting pretty good at yodeling, but there is not a big calling for that.

As I listened to the speaker, he began to say things that caused me to think. He said that God works in mysterious ways and that He cannot use a person who is not willing to give themselves up and take on Christ. Hey! I was willing to give myself up. I didn't like who I was anyway. The problem was that I had an extremely poor outlook on myself. If I couldn't even be grateful for what God had done in my life, how was I going to help others see that they are special to God just the way they are? God had some more work to do on me. I had a long way to go.

Since that day I have learned a lot about God and His love towards me. He really does care about me. He understands the things that I have been through and He still allowed them to happen. He needed me to realize some things before He could really use me. I had to learn to trust Him through everything. Whatever the situation was, I needed to understand that He was still in control. So, now I needed to learn to trust Him and accept His methods of doing things.

————— Do What? —————

Trust is something that comes relatively easy when it deals with trusting in God's love for us. It is something entirely different when God asks us to increase our faith. We all have a comfort zone. Mine is disturbed when I am asked to do anything that brings on an existing or new fear. If God were to ask me to throw myself off a 300 ft. building with no safety devices, while reminding me that He would never leave nor forsake me, I think I would still have issues. Even though He said that He would catch me and I know that He cannot lie, my trust would have to be completely in Him in order for me to do what seems to be the grand-daddy of all stupid ideas.

Although God would never ask us to leap from a building, He does ask us to leap from our comfort zone. It may not be a physical jump we are asked to make. It may be something entirely different. Just read through the Bible. God has always had a way of making people stand in awe with their mouths hanging open, wondering if they just heard Him right.

I love to read through the Bible and put myself in the characters' situations. When you look at the story from the character's perspective it becomes a little more personal. It is hard to imagine what we would do in their position. It was not the ordinary run-of-the-mill kind of stuff that God was asking them to do. He got creative. He found something that was far out of their comfort zone and that's what He decided to approach them with.

God is all powerful and has the ability to control the outcome of any situation. It is our job to realize that, and put total faith in the fact that He has complete control. God's mysterious ways are not new. He has never changed. He has always messed with people even in Bible times.

Take Moses for example. Here's a man that was presented with several bad ideas throughout his life. Moses never asked to be put in the situations he got into. God put him there. When we see him as an adult, he is watching his sheep and minding his own business. God saw this as the perfect opportunity to really freak him out. Off in the distance was a burning bush, or maybe a non-burning bush. It all depends on how you look at it. The bush was on fire, but it was not being consumed. That would be freaky enough all by itself.

If I saw this happening, I would just assume that it was time to pack my things and catch the first bus to the asylum. Moses, on the other hand, thought this was pretty cool and decided that he was going to go take a closer look. This is probably where God smiled, looked at the angels, and said, "We have a live one here. He's going to do fine". Most people would have been home hiding underneath their bed, but not our hero. He was crazy enough to hang around and take a closer look.

There is a slight chance that I may have done the same thing. A non-burning, burning bush would be a little fascinating, but what happened next would have been the clincher. God saw that Moses was crazy enough to start walking over to the bush, so He took the insanity a little farther. From the bush, God started talking. Now we have a non-burning, burning bush that talks. Not only is it talking, but it knows him by name. The first word that came from the bush was, "Moses".

I don't know about you, but if I'm walking up to a non-burning, burning bush and it calls out my name, I'm pulling out a weed-eater and going ballistic. That thing would have said its last word as soon as it had said its first one. Moses took a different approach. When the bush said, "Moses", Moses said, "Here am I". If I felt the need to respond to a talking bush my response would not have been, "Here am I". My response would have been more like, "Yeah, I just saw him a little bit ago. He was on his way to Chicago. Maybe you should go set the Sears Tower on fire and start calling his name."

God was about to do great things with Moses, but Moses felt under-qualified for the job. When God told him that He was going to use him to deliver the children of Israel from Egypt, Moses started reasoning.

This is exactly how we accomplish so little for God. We start thinking for ourselves. What are we going to lose? How will this affect our lives? What will other people think of us? As soon as we throw ourselves into the equation, we start making less room for God. When God says jump, we should not even hesitate long enough to ask Him how high. Just jump. He will take you to heights that you did not even know were possible.

Because Moses began reasoning, God decided it was time to mess with his head in greater ways. Moses started in with his excuses. It was almost as if he had a list prepared just in case this moment should ever arise. Moses fired the first shot. He said that the children of Israel would need to know who sent him. They're not going to follow just anybody. Why would they listen to him? Then God shot back. God told Moses to tell them that "I Am" had sent him.

Well, that pretty much covers all the bases now doesn't it? What better name is there to describe God? "I Am". He is what? Whatever you are in need of – He is. He is a provider, a sustainer, a mediator, a judge, a friend that sticketh closer than a brother, and a God who is totally in love with you and would give anything, including His own life, to be near you. Whatever we need – He is.

Moses was being prepared for great things and his preparation was starting right then. After many excuses God saw the opportunity to use a visual aid. "Moses", He said, "What is that in your hand?" Moses looked at his hand and replied, "A rod." God told him to throw it on the ground. To Moses this didn't seem to be that difficult a task, so he did it.

As soon as that rod hit the ground it became a snake. As soon as that rod turned into a snake, Moses became the new world record holder for the one-hundred meter dash. The Bible says he fled, and I don't blame him at all. This was his trusty rod. It helped him guide the sheep to where they needed to go. Now, it betrays him and turns into a snake. Moses was probably thinking, "That rod cannot be trusted".

Then God asked him to trust it. Actually, He wanted Moses to trust Him. This is where Moses needed to trust God one-hundred percent. God asked him to pick up the snake, but not by the rule of snake handling. The proper way to pick up a snake is to grab it right behind its head. The way God wanted Moses to pick it up was by the tail.

Moses understood the rule of snake handling. He also believed that it was a good rule. If you grab a snake behind its head, the only way it can bite you is if you put your finger in its mouth. In that case, you probably deserve to get bit. Even though it seemed to be a very bad idea, Moses did the unthinkable. He did not think about himself any longer. He thought about obeying God and that's it. When he grabbed the snake like God told him to, it turned back into a rod.

If we do what God tells us to do, everything will turn out alright; even when it seems like it is out of control. God was able to use Moses in a great way because he gave God complete control of his life.

Looking back on my teenage years I can see now that my life was not out of control. It was just not in my control. God will take you through many things in your life. First, you must humble yourself and let Him have His way in your life. You must also realize that He did not make a mistake by making you. You do have a specific purpose. Let God reveal it to you in His time.

God was revealing a few things to me; things that I needed desperately. First, I needed humility. I needed to learn that life was not all about me. Second, I needed to learn to trust Him. It was important for me to realize that God was the one who was in control. Then a new question entered my mind. If God was in control, why did I still feel alone from time to time? He said that He would always be with me. If He was in control, why were there still times in my life when I felt as if there was no control?

Ask Yourself This

— What two things were mentioned in this chapter, that we need to learn?

1. _____

2. _____

— Do I trust God as much as I should?
_____

— If I <u>think about it for a minute</u>; who would I say that I put first in my life....God or myself? _____

Memorize This:

**James 4:10 "Humble yourselves
in the sight of the Lord,
and he shall lift you up."**

**Proverbs 3:5 "Trust in the LORD
with all thine heart; and lean not unto
thine own understanding."**

The Day God Gave Us Control

There are so many things we as humans take for granted. We don't even see how unique God actually made us. The Bible says that we are "*fearfully and wonderfully made*" (Ps. 139:14). We often overlook this fact. Teenagers look past it a lot. I know it's true. I do remember doing it myself. Every time I looked in the mirror I felt a little lower than I felt before I looked in the mirror. My self-image was bad because I did not look at what God had already given me. I was wonderfully made. I was an adult before I realized what this verse actually meant. I do not want you to miss this. It is better for you to realize the truth of this verse as a teenager, than to wait until you are an adult. Right now I want you to stare at this page. Do not blink your eyes or look away. When your eyes start to water, wipe away your tears and continue reading.

(DRAMATIC PAUSE)

What just happened was natural. When your eyes start to get dry you will naturally blink them. If you do not blink them, your eyes will begin to water to keep themselves from drying out. When something gets in your eye it does the same thing. It tries to flush out the intruder. You do not have to tell it to do this. It pretty much reacts without your permission.

You have also been doing something else while you have been reading. You've been breathing in and out. I know — you're asking yourself, "How did he know that?" Could you imagine what life would be like if we had to remind ourselves to breathe? We would all be paranoid, staring off into space, and focusing on our breathing. And may God help the individual that distracts us, even if it's by accident.

Now, granted the average life span would be about twenty-four hours. It's difficult to remind yourself of anything while you are sleeping. Chances are we would also be blind. Who has time to remind their eyes to blink and water when they have to focus on breathing?

So already we would be doomed if God turned control over to us. We would be blind and then dead within twenty-four hours. Actually, we wouldn't even live that long. I know I would be toast if I were left to take care of myself. I would end up getting cut or wounded somehow and would begin to bleed like crazy. I would then have to tell my blood to start clotting to form a scab since it would not do it on its own.

Meanwhile, I would be in a panic because I would need to keep my heart beating; which is causing my blood to keep flowing. Not to mention that the pain could be severe enough to make me cry. Then I would have to tell my tear ducts to release water so that my eyes would not get too dry. In all of this chaos I will definitely need to keep breathing.

Even if someone who was more experienced came to me and started telling me how to control the situation, I would not be able to hear them without telling my ears to listen. Let's just assume they were able to calm me down. They would have me sit down and take deep breaths. Then they would give me a glass of water to drink because my throat would be dry from all of my endless screaming. Soon they would be trying to revive a dead man. As soon as I begin drinking that water I would drown. You see, our tongues rise up when we are drinking. The back of our tongues go up to block the liquid from going down while we swallow what we have just poured down our throat. My eyes would pop wide open when I realize that I had just filled my lungs with water. Then I would be history, because I forgot to tell my body to cough.

Sounds crazy doesn't it? It's true. God has made our bodies to take care of themselves without our help. We must still do our best to take care of our bodies, but without God we are totally helpless. If you have ever seen a newborn baby you can understand a little bit of what I am saying. That child cannot roll over, sit up, or even hold its head up by itself. It cannot go get food, change itself, or talk. Newborn babies are totally helpless. They need someone there for them all of the time. This is a great picture of what God is to us. Without Him we are just like this baby. We need Him. We would never leave a baby in the middle of the floor and expect it to get up and take care of itself. It is the same way with God. He will not leave us alone to fend for ourselves. He will always supply for us. If He left us in control of everything we would die and He knows it. Even though He will not leave us alone to fend for ourselves, there was a day when He gave us complete control.

This control was not the responsibility to control our bodies' functions. It was control of something altogether different. In the middle of designing us in the wonderful way that He did, He also gave us a free will. This free will allows us to make our own choices. I have been told that this is where God made a mistake. Now, because of this free will, we are at risk of going to Hell. God gave us an option to love Him or to reject Him. If we did not have the choice to reject Him there would not be people dying and going to Hell. So, why did God give us this free will? Here's the answer.

God wanted a creature that He could love and that would love Him in return. If we loved Him because that was all we could do, then we wouldn't really love Him. If I were able to come to your house and program a computer to love you, would it really love you? It can only do what I have programmed it to do. It has no choice. Love is all it can do. That is not real love. Love is something you must choose to do. When you love someone it is because you choose them. You were not forced to love them. You love them because of who they are. You didn't have to do it. You chose to.

We had to have an option or there would be no love. The option is to choose Him or to reject Him. I have also been asked why Hell is such a terrible place and why God would send us there. First of all, God doesn't send us there. Remember? We made a choice. If we choose God, we get all that He is. If we choose to reject Him, we get all that the absence of God is. God can be described as *love, joy, peace, longsuffering, gentleness, goodness, faith, meekness, and temperance* (Gal. 5:22-23). This is the fruit of His Spirit. If you take all of that away you will have hatred, fear, pain, suffering, torment, no hope, and everlasting darkness. What you have is the absence of God, better known as "Hell".

Our choice is simple — God or no God. It is up to us. It is not up to Him. God has never been unfair in any way. Because we choose to reject His will from time to time, we have become a sinner. Our sin is what keeps us from going to Heaven. We are all sinners, yet God still loves every one of us. He loved us so much that He allowed His only Son to take our punishment so that we might be saved. Christ was sinless, and was willing to die a sinner's death. He took our place on the cross so that God could see us through His Son. Then He rose again to show us that He could conquer death and Hell. He stands in the gap for us. We could not get to Heaven on our own, so He provided a way. All we have to do is accept His gift, acknowledge the fact that we are sinners in need of a Savior, and accept Him into our lives. He did all of the work. The rest is easy. We just have to make a choice.

Sometimes it is hard to understand why we think we should be able to do what He tells us not to do. Just look at how limited we really are. The very life that is in us is the breath of God. I hope this will help you develop a new and healthier look at who God is. Knowing the position of God in comparison to our role is great, but we are still down here wondering what our purpose is. Without purpose we live an aimless life. I may not know you personally, but I can tell you what your purpose is.

As I have already said, you are being taken through a series of events to be formed into what God has for you. The first step is to realize that we are all sinners in need of a Savior, and accept what He has done for us. If you do not know if you will spend eternity with God in Heaven, I am asking you to think about that right now. It is not worth putting off until later. Please take care of it right now. Ask Him to forgive you of your sins and come into your life.

If you have done that, the next step is to be baptized. This is a command of God — not a suggestion. I just have one recommendation for you. As you are being baptized, remember that you are not completely in control of your body. When I got baptized I forgot to stop breathing when I was put under the water. This forced me into putting on one of the greatest performances of my life. I came up out of the water coughing and gagging in front of the entire church. I'm sure I made my parents extremely proud that day. Their son had attempted what no other church member before him had. He had boldly displayed his intelligence while attempting to breathe under water. Hey, I was only four years old. I didn't know the rules.

Baptism is the first step in obedience after salvation, but we must continue in that obedience by yielding our lives to God — daily. After we give our lives over to God, He will begin working on us, but it is our choice whether or not to give it over to God. Free will is an awesome thing to have, but we must use it wisely. We can either turn the control over to God or we can try to keep it ourselves.

− − − − − Pull Over, Please − − − − −

As you have probably already been able to see, I view life in a different way. Some people see life as a roller coaster ride with its ups and downs. Some see it as a hurricane with them as the only obstacle in its path, and we all know that some see life like a box of chocolates, never knowing what they're going to get. I, however, have an altogether different view of life. I see it as a car and I am the teenager wanting to borrow the keys. Don't have me committed just yet. Allow me to illustrate my messed up point-of-view to you.

When I was a teenager I lost my mind. I know this now because I can look back and see the absence of it. I really didn't know it was missing at the time. My brother, my friend, and I had devised a diabolical plan. We researched the possibilities, checked to see if we had all of the equipment necessary to pull it off, and appointed a specific time to execute this brainless wonder.

After several seconds of careful consideration, we decided that our plan was flawless. We had one large bucket, enough water balloons to get ourselves in serious trouble, and a water balloon launcher. Here is how the plan was supposed to work. We had set our sites on a park about nine blocks away from my house. In this park was a fenced-in basketball court. Every night there would be several teenagers playing basketball in this court. After dark, we decided it would be a lot of fun to hide along the edge of the park and shoot water balloons into the fenced-in court. The people being shot at would not be able to see us, because we would be far enough away and hiding. The plan was to go into the park, shoot water balloons at unsuspecting victims, and go home with the satisfaction that we had pulled it off successfully. That was the plan. That is not how it worked.

When we got to the park we saw that there were several well-built, muscular, senior high boys playing ball. The three of us were freshmen. It did not matter who we were shooting at or how in shape they were. They were never going to see us anyway. We found our place of hiding and began to unload the equipment. We took out the water balloon launcher, which was basically a glorified rubber band with a pouch attached to it. My brother held one end of the rubber band and I held the other. My friend was the one that loaded the balloon into the pouch located in the center of the rubber band. He pulled that pouch back as far as he could, and then let it go. That balloon took off through the air on its mission. A few seconds later we saw it hit the court. The game had suddenly stopped and the players began to look around. They could not figure out where that balloon had come from. This was my life and I was driving. I had the wheel to the car.

These guys could not catch me if they could not see me. We were the ones in charge of this game. They had to play by our rules. We were in control. After a few minutes had passed, they decided to continue on with the game. So did we. We loaded another balloon and let it go. Again, the game was put on hold. They were confused. We still had the wheel. Once we let the third balloon go, my car started giving me trouble.

These guys decided to form a posse and find out who was the one behind these attacks.

Immediately, my brother and my friend climbed up a tree. This tree just happened to be big enough for two people. They were the two, and they were not moving. There was no vacancy for me. As I was looking for a place to hide, those senior high guys took the wheel of my car. I was no longer the one driving. My control was gone. I was suddenly just in it for the ride and I had no idea where they were taking me. Then they clarified it for me. They yelled, "There he is! Let's kill him!" Now, I knew where I was going. I was about to see Jesus face to face and I wasn't sure how I was going to explain the situation to Him when I got there. At that moment my brother spoke a very profound word of wisdom. "Run!" That word relayed a clear message to me. I looked at the posse and decided that I would yield to his advice.

I began to run. The posse began to run faster. I thought that was a good idea, so I did the same. I was now in a fight to get the wheel back. That is when I saw my opportunity. As I turned the corner I discovered a fence, so I jumped it. The wheel was mine again. I had escaped. Then I gave it away again. I had jumped the fence into somebody's back yard. In that back yard was a Rottweiler. Suddenly, I realized that he was behind the wheel. A dog was driving my car. My life was now in the paws of this angry beast. I think his agenda was the same as the guys who were previously chasing me. I was going to see Jesus again.

God was watching the whole thing. He knew about my situation and He reminded me that He did, so I said the shortest prayer of my life. In a soft, squeaky, whispering tone I said, "*Help!*" Then I heard the dog yelp. That Rottweiler no longer had the wheel. He had given it up to a chain. The chain was in control. My life had switched drivers several times in the period of two minutes, and finally; God was back behind the wheel. God told the Rottweiler to lie down and be quiet, and it did. I sat there thinking about how God had just spared me again. I was thankful that He was back behind the wheel. My friend, my brother, and I all left that situation with our lives intact.

Our free will has been given to us by an Almighty God who desires that we use it for Him. He will allow us to try to control our own lives if we want to. But just like my situation with the water balloons, we will find out how little control we actually have. I truly believed I had the upper hand in that situation. I soon found out that the whole event was out of my control.

When we attempt to take control from God, our situation just keeps getting worse. We need to realize that the One who created us is the One who knows what is best for us. He does not want us to try to take control. He wants us to yield it over to Him. When we take charge, we are usually focused on ourselves, and it is difficult for God to use us when we are consumed with self. It took many lessons in my life before I got this message.

I'm going to try to save you the trouble of going through these lessons. **REALIZE NOW THAT YOU ARE NOT SUPPOSED TO BE THE FOCUS OF YOUR LIFE**. When we think about ourselves and what we can get out of life, we begin sinking lower and lower into what Satan has set up for us. He wants us to feel depressed, lonely, and as if no one really cares. I fell into that hole. Many times I would go to my bedroom and cry for hours. I really didn't know why — I just needed to cry. I couldn't share my problems with anyone because I didn't know what they were. I had no one to talk to and nothing to say. I was really depressed. The longer I was depressed the angrier I would get. The angrier I became, the more I took it out on others. I was being unfair to everyone around me. I didn't know what was wrong. I was just unhappy. I got mad about stupid stuff, like finding that we were out of toilet paper after it was too late to rescue my pride. I had a problem building up in my life and I needed a diagnosis.

Ask Yourself This

— Do I want my life to truly count for Christ or myself? _____

— Have I been using my free will to glorify God or not? _____

— Am I willing to completely turn my life over to Him? _____

— Do I believe that God is pleased with how I live my life? _____

Memorize This:

Rom. 6:13 "Neither yield ye your members as instruments of unrighteousness unto sin: but yield yourselves unto God, as those that are alive from the dead, and your members as instruments of righteousness unto God."

Doctor We Have No "Patience"

God had been teaching me many lessons in my life. Every one of them was helping me get closer to understanding what I needed to be. But class wasn't dismissed yet. He also saw that I needed the most irritating lesson of life taught to me. It was the lesson of patience. This lesson was one I was not prepared for. I did not even see that I needed patience. I wasn't the one with the problem. Frustrating things were just happening to me. It wasn't like I could make them stop. Everyone has irritations. Mine were just happening more frequently than before.

God diagnosed me with the lack of patience, and there was only one cure. Romans 5:3 says that *"tribulation worketh patience"*. This is a tough fact, but it is true. Tribulations are things that happen in our lives that we feel we can do without. God allows them to happen so that we can learn valuable lessons like patience.

The reason I lost my patience in the first place was because of my self-esteem. When you feel like a loser you begin to dislike yourself, and a person who dislikes who they are eventually becomes irritable. I did not understand why everything and everybody was getting on my nerves. I had turned into an angry young man. I wasn't stupid though. I knew that this behavior was unacceptable, but everything was starting to bug me.

I remember getting mad when I walked through my room barefooted, while carrying a stack of clothes to put away. I stepped on a piece of paper that loved me and didn't want to see me go. I shook my foot around with all the energy I had, and it still remained attached to the bottom of my sweaty foot. I then had to put down what I was holding to take the love sick refuse from my foot. After I forced it to leave me alone, I was free to walk again. I picked up my stuff and proceeded on with my journey through the room. On my way back through, the love sick paper struck again. It had a hold of me and it was happy to follow me wherever I went. I didn't want to be followed. This time I got mad. I threw the clothes I was holding and reached down to grab the friendly intruder. I wadded him up and chucked him across the room. Then I realized that I had to pick up all of my clothes and re-fold them. I was aggravated. God knew what was going on, and again, He completely approved.

Many other things happened to me. It seemed as if irritation was looking for me on a daily basis. I started to snap at people when they really didn't do anything wrong. Then they would get mad at me for snapping at them. I found that if you snap at people enough, they do not want to be around you much. Before you know it, you have been sucked into that trap Satan has set up again. Once again you are alone.

I had to overcome this problem, so I turned to the One who had the answers — God. It's a shame that God is usually our last resort. The one person we should go to immediately is the one we go to last. If anyone is going to understand what we are going through, it is the one who made us. I had no where else to turn.

Reading my Bible is something I had not done in awhile, so I picked it up. I turned to Romans because it is the book most people tell you to read when you get saved. I had been saved for a while, but I felt like I was starting over in my Christian walk. That's when God showed me the answer to my problem. There it was — the one thing I had been looking for. Romans 5:3 was staring me in the face. *"Tribulation worketh patience"*.

God was trying to teach me patience, but I was failing the class over and over again because I was not doing my part. Just because God wants you to have something does not mean you are going to get it. It all comes down to our free will. If we do not accept what God is trying to teach us, it will take longer for us to learn it. I had to realize that all of these little irritations in my life were there to help me develop patience.

I knew I needed to learn patience, so I made up my mind that I would handle the frustrations differently. When things started to drive me crazy, I would just pause and think of how stupid it would be to get upset about it. I had made up my mind. I was going to overcome this. God saw my plan and He agreed that it was a good one. Once I had made up my mind to change, I thought the irritations would lessen. Actually, the opposite happened. They doubled.

Now I couldn't turn the corner without things happening to me. Seriously, I felt like I was sweating sugar in a room covered with ants. The harder I tried to get away from them, the more sugar I would sweat out. These irritation ants would not leave me alone. The only way to get rid of the irritation ants was with the insecticide of self-control and I knew it. I had to calmly deal with each frustration. I was doing fine at first. I would remind myself that these little things were not a big deal. Finally, I felt like I was getting a handle on my life. Then God took me to Patience 102.

− − − − − **Messenger Pigeons** − − − − −

Somewhere in my past I must have messed with the wrong bird. This was not just any bird I had rubbed the wrong way. This bird was part of the "flying mafia". Whatever I did to upset this little guy caused him to fly home and tell Uncle Guido, who in turn called the rest of the group. The flying mafia was in my neighborhood and I was the mark.

I was walking into the church building one Sunday when the mafia found me. I was almost to the porch of the church when Uncle Guido flew over me. He was flying in the opposite direction that I was walking. The shot was fired. Guido was an excellent marksman. Before I even knew they were in town, I had a flowing stream of pigeon bullets running down my face. I was hit right between the eyes. These birds knew what they were doing. My first instinct was to get mad. Then I remembered — it was only a test that God was putting me through. I thought about it for a minute. Then one of my friends walked up and saw me standing there in all my glory. When he saw the bird bullet on my face, he began to laugh hysterically. When he started laughing, I did something I had never done when faced with irritation. I lost it. This time I did not lose it in a bad way. I started to laugh uncontrollably. Then another friend saw me in my predicament, and that contagious laughter came over him also. That did not help me get over my uncontrollable laughter though. Usually I would get upset about the fact that they were laughing at me. This time I saw it from their point of view. It was hilarious. I was about to walk into church wearing bird dukie.

Try to think back to what I said at the beginning of this book. It is usually easy to find someone else's bad luck funny. That day I learned how to put myself in the other person's shoes. Seeing my situation from the outside left me with no choice but to appreciate the humor of it all. Sure, it was humbling and a little embarrassing, but what was I going to do? Getting mad was not going to change anything. I just had to deal with it.

Frustrations did not stop coming at me. The difference now was the way I chose to handle them. Not as many things would frustrate me like they used to. I had learned patience. Now when I was faced with tedious projects or irritating people, I was able to remain calm. For the first time in my teenage years I felt like I had a little bit of worth. This feeling of worth did not come to me because of what I did. It came to me because of what I allowed God to do. I let Him guide me. I gave up on my own techniques to make myself a better person. When others looked at me I still didn't appear to be much, but I was starting to feel better about myself. First, I needed to become humble. I had to realize that I was not what the universe revolved around. Then I needed to trust that God had control. Then it was patience. When the tests of humility started to frustrate me and make me feel like a loser, God sent the test of patience. I still could not do a whole lot, but I was okay with that now.

I had come to the point in my life where I was able to look at others rather than myself. I was also able to calmly deal with my problems rather than blow up when they came. For the first time in my life, I realized that I was nothing without Christ. I told you that there was a difference between being a "Nobody" and being "God's Nobody". Any teenager can look at themselves at some time and think of themselves as a "Nobody", but that is not a healthy outlook on life. That is exactly where Satan wants you to be.

When you feel insignificant, you become depressed and lonely. Sometimes you may even go to your room and cry for hours, not even knowing why. It breaks my heart when I hear that another teenager has taken his or her own life because they hated themselves. They felt alone and believed that there was no one who cared for them, so they took their own life to get away from that feeling. Listen! I was there. I felt that feeling. The reason I sat down one day and started writing this book is because I remember what that felt like, and I wanted to show you that it is something you can conquer.

God never wants us to feel insignificant. He wants us to realize that He loved us enough to send His own Son to make a way so that we would not have to spend eternity without Him. In order for Him to let His own Son die in your place, He had to have a divine plan for you; a plan that only you can accomplish. He saw the potential you have, and He fell in love with who you are. There is no way that you are insignificant if God himself would give so much to save you. You have a purpose, and that purpose is to become what God has put you on this earth to become.

That's right, one day He put you here on this earth with an assignment to do. He was there when you were born, and He has been watching you grow up ever since. He has provided for you and has taken care of you up to this very day. You have the undivided attention of God himself. He is watching over you even now as you are reading this book. He loves you and wants you to understand why He has put you here. You are not insignificant. If you were, then God would not have an interest in you, but He does. Let me show you now who God wants you to become.

Ask Yourself This

— Do I allow things to get to me more than I should? _____

— Am I willing to take the time to deal with frustrations the way I believe God would have me to deal with them? _____
_____

— Am I willing to start each day by asking God to remind me to be patient? _____

Memorize This:

Romans 5:3 "And not only so, but we glory in tribulations also: knowing that tribulation worketh patience…"

Roaches
and Holiness

If you can set all of your feelings about yourself to the side and focus on what I am about to say, I think you will begin to understand what I am talking about when I say that there is a way out of that feeling of insignificance. Right now I want you to do something a little out of the ordinary. I want you to try to look at life from a different perspective. You are no longer the "nobody" that sits all alone wondering why you even exist. Now you are the person approaching God and seeking His purpose in your life; willing to yield yourself completely to His will. You are no longer focused on yourself and how you feel. You are now focused on God and what He desires you to be. It is not about you any more. It is about God.

If you would, take a moment right now and ask God to help you understand what He wants for you in your life. Ask Him to help you put yourself to the side and focus on Him. I really want you to see how you can be transformed from a "nobody" into "God's nobody". The only way that you can truly see this is if you are serious about wanting to be what He wants you to be. If you are ready to throw all of the baggage of the past away, and you are serious about focusing on God rather than on self, please take a moment to ask Him to open your eyes to His will.

I hope you have just asked God to help you understand what He wants for you. Without getting Him involved with this, you are trying to do it on your own. Remember, we need Him. It is not your will you should be seeking — it is His will. Like I said before, you do have control of what you will do right now. God gave us all a free will. Use it now to seek understanding. If you are ready to learn about God's purpose for your life, then open your mind to what He wants you to know and read on.

Before we go on any farther, I want to remind you of a few things God needed me to understand. These are things I have already told you, but I do not want you to miss them. First, God needed me to learn to trust Him. Like Moses, we must be willing to obey God to the fullest. When you realize His purpose for your life, you must be willing to obey Him and trust Him, even if His command seems difficult to follow. (Proverbs 3:5 *"Trust in the LORD with all thine heart; and lean not unto thine own understanding. In all thy ways acknowledge him, and he shall direct thy path."*)

Second, I had to learn that I was nothing on my own. I had to realize that without God I could do nothing (**John 15:5**). He is our "everything". Once

I caught on to that idea, it only made sense to give my life over to Him completely. Plus, I really wasn't doing such a great job on my own anyway.

The third thing that I needed to learn was self-control. How can we ever help somebody else if we cannot even control ourselves? I had to learn patience and accept that when bad things happened, it was just something that would make me stronger if I handled it in the right way.

There are many lessons that we all will have to learn in our lives. The willingness to learn them will make it easier on us. The way to make sure that we learn the lessons God has for us is to always seek His will in everything we do. Now that I have said all of that, let's make the title of this chapter make sense.

————— The Roach Approach —————

We all know what roaches are, but do we understand what true holiness is? In **1 Peter 1:16** God tells us to be holy. That is not a suggestion –it's a command. God has given us a command to follow. Now we have a purpose. We are to follow out this command. The funny thing about a command is that the person receiving it must first understand what it is.

Allow me to illustrate this for you. Let's imagine that I have asked you to do me a favor. I have asked you to go to my house and check the items with the "xylems". You are more than willing to help me. Immediately, you take off and head for my house, jumping over fences and dodging traffic. When you get there you are exhausted, but you are on a mission and you won't stop until it is carried out. Then you realize there is a problem. Which item is it that has the "xylem"? Never mind that. What in the world is a "xylem"?

As you are standing there, you realize you are not able to carry out my request because of the lack of information. I had never explained that a xylem was part of a flower. I guess I could have said the word "flower", but that would have really ruined this illustration altogether. Now, you are at my house with a purpose that you cannot fulfill.

God has both given us all a purpose and the information that we need to fulfill that purpose. He has not hidden anything from us. He wants us to be like His Son. We are to model our lives after Jesus Christ, who is holy. We are to be holy, for He is holy. So what is holiness? If you were to try to answer this question without reading any farther, you might give an answer like faith or good works. These are common answers to this question, but they are incorrect.

If faith were holiness, then God would not have to tell us to be holy. You see, we had to have faith in order to accept the fact that Jesus Christ was God's Son. We would also need faith to pray and believe that God hears our prayers. If faith were holiness, then many of us already have it — even if it is just a little bit.

If good works were what holiness was, then most of us would have it. Everyone does good works from time to time, but doing good works does not make us holy. So, if good works and faith are not what holiness is, then what is it? Let me give you my definition of what holiness really is.

Right now, I would like you to picture yourself walking down the stairs into a dark, cold basement. As you reach the last few steps, the light burns out. Now you are forced to use the flashlight, which you have with you. The flashlight is giving you trouble, so you tap it on your hand to get it to work. As you are focusing on the flashlight, you lose your balance and tumble down the remaining steps. You fall on your face onto the basement floor. As soon as you hit the floor, you hear a crunching noise and you sense something crawling on you. Right then, the flashlight comes on and you see something that you are not prepared for. The entire basement is covered with roaches.

You shine your light to the floor, and it seems as if the floor is moving. Now you know that the crunching sound you heard earlier was your face squishing these little creatures against the floor. You feel your face with your hand and the slime is overwhelming. Then you feel an even more disturbing sensation. Something is moving around in your mouth.

You try to spit it out but its legs are caught in your teeth. You want to reach in and grab it, but you discover that your hands are covered with them also. Panic starts to set in and you scream. Now you have accidentally bitten into the bug. The juices are filling your mouth and you are feeling ill. All you can do is try to get out of this bug-infested trap. You run up the stairs, smashing roaches all the way. Finally, you have reached the top. You slam the basement door and slide down the wall until you are sitting on the floor.

Then you feel it again. This time the roach is not in your mouth. It is in your ear and it is trying to dig deeper and deeper into it. As you reach into your ear to pull it out, you grab onto one of its legs. You pull on it, but the unexpected happens. The roach's leg comes off and you feel the ooze starting to run down the side of your face.

Now that is just disgusting! What in the world does this story have to do with holiness? Well, I'm glad you asked. When you can look at sin the same way you look at these roaches, you have achieved holiness. When you can look at sin and have that feeling that you want nothing to do with it, then you will understand what holiness is. This is something each of us must strive for in our lives. It should be our desire to be more like Christ. Sin is what separates us from God. Holiness is to turn away from sin and to choose God instead.

Every time we decide to go towards sin, we walk farther away from God. The farther we get from God, the lonelier we become. That is when we fall into that depressed state where we feel insignificant. I believe you know exactly what I am talking about. It is when we begin to feel like a "nobody".

Let's do the math. God created us to have a relationship with Him. One day we broke that relationship by sinning. So far, we see that people + sin = separation from God. God then supplied the answer to this problem. He sent His Son into the equation to bring us back to God. Now we have a new answer. People + Jesus = a relationship with God. Finally, our relationship is mended. But, just like every difficult math problem another piece is added to make it harder to figure out the answer. Satan wants to be in the math class too. After we are saved and our relationship has been mended, Satan throws in a few wrenches to complicate the problem. He tries to get us to sin.

Remember what it was that broke our relationship with God in the first place? That's right — sin. Whatever you do, remember that once God has given you the gift of eternal life through His Son, He will not take that away from you. He promised to give you everlasting life. This was not based on our good works. Ephesians 2:8-9 says, "*For by grace are ye saved through faith; and that not of yourselves: it is the gift of God: Not of works, lest any man should boast".*

Everlasting life was paid for by the blood of Jesus. There is nothing that you can do to get yourself to Heaven, and once you are saved, there is nothing you can do to lose your salvation. In John 6:38-40 Jesus said, *"For I came down from heaven, not to do mine own will, but the will of him that sent me. And this is the Father's will which hath sent me, that of all which he hath given me I should lose nothing, but should raise it up again at the last day. And this is the will of him that sent me, that every one which seeth the Son, and believeth on him, may have everlasting life: and I will raise him up at the last day."*

The reason that Satan wants us to sin is not so that we will lose our salvation. He knows that can't be done. He wants us to sin because it draws us farther away from God's will, or in other words, God's purpose for our lives. If we do not seek God's purpose in our lives then we seek our own. Yes, this can be fulfilling for a while, but the only way to fill that God shaped void in our lives is to keep it filled with the things of God. After we get saved we can still choose to sin. If we choose to sin, we put up a wall in our relationship with God. We are still His children. We just hurt the relationship. We need to immediately ask Him to forgive us. If our relationship is not what it should be with God, then we will not accomplish what He wants us to do. Satan now has us back to that lonely feeling again.

The reason God wants us to be holy is simple. When we turn away from sin, we turn to Him. He is also protecting us by warning us about sin and its consequences. He does have our best interest in mind. God loves us so much. Why shouldn't we do our best to please Him? We need to understand how to truly fall in love with Him. Let me explain the kind of love that I am talking about.

Ask Yourself This

— Am I willing to strive to be holy?
_____

— It is important to seek God's will for every day. Am I willing to spend time seeking His will by reading His Word and praying daily? _____

— Do I really want to have a sold-out life for Christ? _____

— What will I do to achieve a sold-out life for Him? _____

Memorize This:

1Peter 1:15-16 "But as he which hath called you is holy, so be ye holy in all manner of conversation; because it is written, be ye holy; for I am holy."

Puppy Love
Is True Love

Let me start out by saying that I really do believe "puppy love" is true love. I know, many people say that it is not really love at all. I just think that there is a misunderstanding. I not only think that it is true love, but that it is one of the truest forms of love. I guess there are two ways of looking at it. It can be seen as a disease or it can be seen the way that I see it. Right now, let's look at it the first way. This is the true definition of "puppy love".

The statistics are overwhelming. Every year thousands of people become victims of this disease called "puppy love". It is not a disease you can feel progressing slowly. There are not a series of stages you encounter with this disease. The only way you can know that you have it is if you are already over-taken by it.

Once you have this disease, you can do nothing to fight it. On the other hand, there is nothing that you want to do about it. It is kind of nice to be sick like this. "Puppy love" is a feel good disease. You never want it to end. This illness is not something that attacks one specific organ in your body. It takes over entirely. Let me tell you how this infection progresses.

First, it attacks your eyes. One minute you are walking around, minding your own business and the next minute you are caught in a trance. You are convinced that you are looking at a piece of heaven. God has placed the perfect person before your very eyes. Then the infection spreads farther. Your mouth has been affected too. It starts to open slowly. Now, you are staring at "Heaven" while your mouth is hanging open. No, it doesn't look intelligent, but you don't care. You're "in love". Now your heart is beating faster and your legs are getting weak. Right then, this heavenly being begins to leave.

As this angel starts to walk away, the plague takes over your mind. Whatever you were doing before is no longer on your to-do list. All you need to do is follow. Your eyes are still focused on this "too-perfect-to-be-human" person. Your mouth is still hanging open and your weak legs are carrying you in the same direction your beating heart is telling them to go. You are determined to follow this love to the ends of the earth. You have been captured by "puppy love".

I remember falling in "puppy love". Remember the girl I told you about in the second chapter? Well, she wasn't my only case of "puppy love". I got sick — constantly. As soon as I recovered from one case of it, I went out to find another case. I was addicted. I wanted to be sick. I had the greatest illness known to man. I didn't even feel sick.

The worst part about "puppy love" is the fact that you do not feel sick until it is gone. It is not even a disease that lasts very long. Soon after you catch the "puppy love" virus, you are healed. It is all over and you feel miserable. This misery you are enduring feels like it will never end. You were determined to follow this "love" to the end of the world and now you are there.

As time goes by, you begin to feel better. Life is getting back to normal. Then you think about that "heavenly" being again. Suddenly, you realize how un-heavenly they really were. You also realize that your "puppy love" wasn't really true love at all. That's right! It was an impostor! This masked disease made its way into your heart and took it for all it was worth. You were scammed! It wasn't even true love.

I know, I told you that "puppy love" was true love and now I'm saying that it isn't. It might sound as if I am changing my story, but I'm not. What I just described to you is the true definition of "puppy love". With that definition anyone can understand how it is not true love. It is just an impostor. It may feel like love, but it's not.

The reason people refer to this disease as "puppy love," is because it is that same feeling that you get when you see a puppy. That cute little ball of fur steals your heart. All you want to do is take it home with you. This phenomenon is called "love at first sight", better known as "puppy love". Before you know it, the puppy is in your house, and he makes himself right at home.

Soon your shoes become chew toys and your floor becomes the "Land of a Thousand Lakes". As you get dressed in the morning, you find yourself running around the house wearing one sock, while your puppy plays "Keep Away" with the other one. You're running late — your puppy is just running. You have priorities. The puppy has your sock. This little footwear game continues for several minutes. You finally retrieve the sock. You have won! At least you thought you did. Suddenly, you realize that you are holding a soggy piece of cotton tubing with a hole on each end. Life is getting ridiculous.

As time goes by, your puppy starts to turn into a dog. On his journey to adulthood, you begin to see strange behavioral tendencies. Your dog has lost its mind. Instead of drinking the water that you have provided, he would rather get his thirst quenched from the toilet. It seems as if his goal in life is to empty this porcelain treasure chest. Every time you turn around, you see him taking another plunge. Soon after this series of sewer slurping, your dog gets the desire to go outside. You realize that you need to grant his wish, otherwise, the "Land of a Thousand Lakes" will be back. So, you let him go outside to take care of this problem.

You now see something that is totally bizarre. Your dog is searching for the perfect spot. This can't be possible. You know he has just consumed at least a gallon of water. If he waits too much longer he will explode. This is no time to be picky. Fifteen minutes later, your dog has taken care of the problem. He heads back towards you. As he is walking back, you marvel at him. You are standing in awe, and he looks extremely happy with drool pouring from his mouth. What happened to your dog?

When he finally reaches you, he discovers something. He is being followed. Something is standing right behind him. Curiosity overwhelms him. At the same time, you begin to wonder what is going through his head. Now your eyes are glued to this animal. What is he doing? He slowly tries to sneak up on this stranger, but the stranger moves away. With every step he makes, the stranger goes faster, but he is determined to catch it. He thinks it is a stalker. You know that it's his tail. The chase is on. The dog picks up speed. He is now running rapidly in circles.

That's when you remember that he was drooling like a faucet. As he chases his tail the drool begins to fly. You are standing beside a sprinkler system that won't stop. This is disgusting. You are wearing doggie drool, and the doggie is continuing to supply it. The "puppy love" is gone.

— — — — — Now For Spot's View — — — — —

Well, now you know. That is why it is called "puppy love." At first sight it seems like love. Then time reveals that it is not. It is just an illusion. I do agree that this is not love at all, but that is not the view of "puppy love" that I would like to talk to you about. The view that I want you to see comes from the puppy.

Even though these canine wonders can be very irritating from time to time, there is still something extremely fascinating about them. It is not just for any reason that the dog is considered to be "man's best friend". There is a special quality about most dogs that we should all consider applying to our own lives. They have "puppy love".

I have a dog named Killer. When people approach our door, Killer immediately begins to bark. As they come closer, Killer growls with disapproval. Ready to tear them from limb to limb, Killer watches as we open the door to let them in. When our guests walk through the door, Killer backs off in fear. You see, Killer is a long-haired Chihuahua. She weighs about four-and-a-half pounds and she is afraid of everything. If you try to pick her up before she has gone outside she will leave a puddle on the floor. She is basically worthless.

I have watched her run away from leaves that were being blown around. When I call her to me, she comes in the manner of a marine crawl. She gets down low on the floor and inches her way towards me. She makes it look as if I have abused her in the past or something. When she stands on her back legs she barely reaches my knee. I'm not yet sure if she is a dog or a guinea pig. I do think it is hilarious that she is so timid. That is why we named her Killer. It's funny.

Although my dog is worthless, she does have one quality that makes her great. The other day I wanted to try out an experiment on her. I laid down on my bed and called her. "Come here Killer." She came to my feet and stopped. So I said it again, "Come here Killer." She climbed up onto my legs and stopped at my knees. I called her again. She stopped at my stomach. I realized what was happening and acknowledged the fact that it was my turn to call her again. So I did. She rested at my neck with her chin on mine. Then my curiosity got the best of me. I started to wonder what she would do if I called her one more time. She was already resting her chin on my chin, but I called her again anyway. This time she stepped up onto my face and plopped down on my mouth. Needless to say, I was done calling her.

The reason I just told you this story about my cute, little worthless dog was to explain "puppy love" from her perspective. Every time I called her she came closer to my call. She had one thing on her mind. She wanted to please me. She was willing to do whatever I asked of her. Her agenda was to do my will. That is why dogs are considered to be man's best friend.

My dog will follow me when I leave a room. When I sit down on the couch she jumps up to be with me. When my wife and I go to bed we can rest assured that Killer is, or soon will be, sleeping next to us. When we leave the house we can hear her cry. Everywhere we go she wants to be there too. She just wants to be in our presence at all times.

Why do dogs want to please us so much? Why do they long to be near their masters? The answer is simple. They love us. They have a love that goes beyond the love that we show them. After a while people get very busy in life and forget about their dogs. The dog, on the other hand, does not forget about us. They are waiting eagerly to be near us again. When we come home they are excited to see us. We mean everything to them. They treasure us.

What would happen in your life if you fell in love with God like this? A dog doesn't worry about who they are or where they are going in life. They just live to please their master. Even though we should make goals for our futures, we cannot forget about our Master. He deserves to be our "everything". But first, we need to see Him for who He is.

I have many abilities that my dog does not have. I am taller, smarter, and stronger. I can also do many things that she cannot do. I go to the store and buy the food for her. I open the bag of food. I get her water from the faucet. Because she lacks the gift of opposable thumbs, she cannot do these things. She relies on me. If my wife and I were to stop caring for her, she would die. She would be stuck in our house without the ability to get food or water. Without us she cannot survive. She needs us and she knows it.

Well, let's face the facts. We are nothing without God. It is true that all of the blessings we have in our lives come from Him. James 1:17 says, *"Every good gift and every perfect gift is from above, and cometh down from the Father of lights, with whom is no variableness, neither shadow of turning".* He truly is the Master. But that's not the question, is it? Is He your Master? Have you come to the point in your life where you can see Him for who He really is? The very life that we have comes from Him. Why shouldn't He get our whole heart, soul, mind, and strength? Isn't that what He tells us to do? Mark 12:30 says, *"And thou shalt love the Lord thy God with all thy heart, and with all thy soul, and with all thy mind, and with all thy strength...."* He deserves it.

Trying to make an image for ourselves is a waste of time. We need to magnify the image of God. If

93

we turn into someone who can entertain the world, we will be loved. If we are able to get to the top of the popularity list, we will be loved. If we give gifts to the world's entire population, we will be loved. But if the world can see the love that we have in our lives for God, there is a good chance that He will be loved. They will see something in our lives that they are missing. All that we can offer the world through ourselves will not last for eternity, but what God can give to the world, through us, will.

We need to be more like man's best friend. We should long to be in the presence of God. Our desire should be to spend time with Him. We should always strive to please Him in everything we do. When He calls, we should come. When He tells us to go, we should go. He deserves to be everything to us. It is a shame that most people worship God when they go to church on Sunday and Wednesday, but they do not even think about Him on the days between those services. We all know that in order to make a relationship stronger we must spend time with the person that we are trying to get to know better. It is the same way with God. If we want to get closer to Him, it will take more than just seeing Him twice a week. Go to His house —the church — but make sure He gets to come to yours also. Fall in love with Him. Matthew 6:21 says, *"For where your treasure is, there will your heart be also."* Is He your treasure?

Ask Yourself This

— Have I been making God first priority in my life? _____

— Am I willing to make Him first priority from this day forward? _____

— How can I show Him that I love Him? (John 14:15) _____

—Am I willing to make a commitment to spend personal time with Him each day?

_____

Memorize This:

Mark 12:30 "And thou shalt love the Lord thy God with all thy heart, and with all thy soul, and with all thy mind, and with all thy strength: this is the first commandment."

Identity
Crisis

*"I have gone out to find myself.
If I should return while I'm away,
please keep me here until I get back."*

I really don't have any idea who thought that saying up, but I can't think of a better way to describe what an identity crisis is. Your identity is who you are. The main problem we have when we feel like a "Nobody" is that we do not really have an identity. We don't know who we are or what our purpose is. Your purpose is to glorify God by giving your all for Christ. That truly is your purpose. Many other things go along with that purpose, but that is the general idea.

We all need an image. I understand that. Without an identity we don't exist. We all need to find an identity in something. If you watch children for any length of time, you will see that they go from one identity one day, to another identity the next. One

99

day they are Indiana Jones running through a tunnel to escape from a giant boulder. The next day they are leaping tall buildings in a single bound. It is usually an exciting identity that they choose to be.

You will probably never hear a child argue to be the guy who scrubs the hero's toilet. Can you imagine a line of children with their hands folded in front of them, praying silently to be picked for this part? Yeah, me neither. Everybody wants to be some-body cool. No one wants to be a "nobody". Yet the crazy guy who wrote this book is trying to get you to become a "Nobody", but not just any "Nobody" — "God's nobody". Still, you need an identity. What does a "Nobody" that belongs to God do?

Your identity will come when you understand what God's will is for your life. Here is where it gets a little weird. God has two purposes for your life. Yep, you read it right; two of them. He has a general purpose for you, and He has a specific purpose for you. One of them you will get NOW. The other, you will get after that. Are you supposed to be a great public speaker that reaches thousands of souls for Christ every day? Are you to be on a missions team that goes all over the world to help existing mission-aries? Maybe you are just supposed to be that person who faithfully shows up to church every service to welcome the other people as they arrive. If you are at the point in your life that you just want to know God's will, all of these possibilities probably sound okay. You just want to know what your purpose on this earth is.

Well, I've got good news and bad news for you. The good news is that God wants you to know His will for your life <u>right now</u>. The bad news is that you will need to wait to know His will for your life until after you first do His will.

Oh great, he's totally lost it. Up to this point, it looked as if we might have been going somewhere. Now we are lost in oblivion with a crazy guy with an unusually stupid bad news, good news scenario. To know what God's will is for our lives, we must first do His will. What is that supposed to mean? That is like saying, "If you want directions to my house, please come to my house and get them." How are we supposed to do God's will before we know what it is? That's just insane.

Alright, I know it sounds like I am just talking until I think of something to say, but it actually makes sense. Remember, I did say that He has two purposes for you. His first purpose, or will for our lives is His general will. 1 Thessalonians 4:3 says, *"For this is the will of God, even your sanctification...."* Sanctification means "set apart". After we get saved, God wants us to live a holy life that is set apart for Him. We are to be an example for the entire world to see.

Satan has blinded the eyes of so many people. They need to see Christ living through us. There has to be something different. They must see that we have something that they are missing. Then they will be drawn closer to Christ by the lives we live. God's will for your life right now is to do what is morally right. You are to be building a relationship with Him. The better your relationship is with Him, the more you trust Him and are willing to do whatever He asks of you.

Let's imagine that you have money. I know; we are really stretching for an illustration this time. Let's just try to imagine it anyway. A good friend of yours approaches you and asks you a bizarre question. Keep in mind that this is a good friend of yours. He wants you to give him your fifty-thousand dollar, one-of-a-kind, can-help-you-see-through-walls and help-you-fly, cell phone. He tells you that he needs you to loan it to him for one hour, but he can't tell you why. You know he is honest and will not do anything illegal with it. You also know that within the hour you will have it back in your hands in the same condition you loaned it to him in. So you go ahead and give it to him.

Scenario two: A big burly man, covered in tattoos and scars, approaches you with the same question. You do not know this dude. But, hey, you're a trusting individual, right? You would probably just hand that cool little cell phone over to him with a smile, wouldn't you? No, I don't think so. You don't know him. You don't trust him. You never built a relationship with him. How can he actually expect you to do what he asks if he has not built a trusting relationship with you? He may be telling you the truth, but you are not going to do his will because you don't know him well enough.

That is exactly what you are dealing with when it comes to God. How can He give you His specific will for your life before you have even built a relationship with Him? He does want you to know His specific will, but you need to do His general will first. Talk with Him, listen to Him by reading His Word, talk to others about Him, and grow to love Him more and more each day. If you do this, He will approach you with a request one day that you will be more than happy to do because of the trusting relationship you have with Him. You build that relationship by seeking to please Him every day of your life. Then you will be introduced to His specific will.

We often spend so much time trying to discover God's specific purpose for our lives that we do not work on our relationship with Him. The truth is, the closer we get to Him, the better we will be able to serve Him in the position He places us in later. Maybe He has already placed a burden on your heart for a specific group of people. Maybe He has already told you what your specific purpose is, but in order to complete that purpose you must keep your relationship pure with Him.

Your responsibility is not to worry about your specific purpose in life. Your responsibility is to live for, and please your Savior right now. Your specific purpose in life is coming. You don't need to worry about that. God does not want to keep it from you. The only thing you need to focus on right now is whether or not you are living a life for Him like you should. If we cannot be faithful with the little things, why are we expecting more? Do what is right because it is right. He will be pleased. I promise.

Ask Yourself This

— Am I willing to do what I know is right?

_____

— Can others truly see Christ in me? _____

_____

— Is my relationship with Christ all that it should be? _____

— What is my general purpose in life?

_____

Memorize This:

Colossians 3:17 "And whatsoever ye do in word or deed, do all in the name of the Lord Jesus, giving thanks to God and the Father by him."

It's Not
My Life
It's My Turn

It is going to seem like we have switched tracks for a little bit, but trust me. This is the same book and I am the same guy writing it. I want to make sense out of this chapter's title also. No, this one is not about disgusting little bugs. It is about you. If you are currently feeling like a "nobody" or have a tendency to do so, this chapter may make things a little bit clearer to you.

During the war in Iraq, America heard of how several of our soldiers were being abused by the enemy. Many Americans sat around their televisions and watched as the news poured in of how American soldiers and civilians were being taken captive. The terrorists had no mercy on our P.O.W's whatsoever. They would not only torture them, but they would also kill them in inhumane ways. This same kind of people flew two planes into our trade towers, one into our Pentagon, and one came down near Somerset, Pennsylvania.

So often we ask ourselves how people could do such heinous crimes and still be able to lay their heads down and sleep at night. What makes a person become like that? Sure, they say it is to please their god, but they do know it is wrong. They know they would not want those things to happen to them, so why would they do it to other people who feel pain, have families, and are human just like them? The answer is simply that they have used their free will to allow Satan to have a strong influence on their lives.

This is not a new type of person that has emerged over the last few years though. This type of person has been around for quite some time. Remember Paul? No, not your friend down the street — the apostle. The apostle Paul was one of the great men of God in the Bible. God used him to write over half the New Testament. Paul preached the gospel of Jesus Christ to the poor and to royalty.

If you were to ask most Christians which Bible character was the greatest servant of God, the majority would answer – "Paul." Outside of Jesus Christ, I would want to make Paul the apostle a man I would pattern my life after. He lived for God with all that he had. Not only did he live his life for God, he died for Him also. Though he was thrown into prison, stoned, beaten, and left for dead, he still got up time and time again to proclaim the gospel of Jesus Christ. But that wasn't always who Paul was.

Before he met Christ and received Him as his personal Savior, Paul was the enemy of Christ. Paul was just like these men we just talked about. He lived to see Christians be put to death. He watched them take their very last breath after being stoned, and then he went after others. He was a cruel man with no desire to live for Christ.

What in the world would make a man like this turn into one of the greatest apostles of all time? How could a man who sought to kill so many Christians become a man that so many Christians claim as a role model? Something big had to have happened. Yes, Paul got saved, but there must have been something else that made this transformation possible.

When we get saved, it is true that the old things in our lives pass away. God said in 2 Corinthians 5:17 *"Therefore if any man be in Christ, he is a new creature: old things are passed away; behold, all things are become new"*. This transformation happens to every one who gets saved, but Paul went a step farther. I have seen many people truly get saved and show the evidence of it in their lives. Paul did something that most don't do though. He went from being someone who lived to defy Christ, to someone who lived to magnify Christ. Just because we get saved does not mean we are going to live a sold out life for God like Paul did. Paul realized something most of us have never realized. He even told us what it was on more than one occasion. In 1Cor. 15:31 Paul said, *"I die daily"*. In Philippians 1:21 he said, *"For* *to me to live is Christ, and to die is gain"*. No, this does not mean that Paul enjoyed dying so much that he did it all the time. That's just crazy. Even though that would be a cool party trick, it is not what he was talking about.

Paul saw the big picture. You see, God did not accidentally put you on this earth in the wrong era. You were not supposed to be born in the middle ages or during the time of the dinosaurs. I know — I want to see one too. God put you on this earth at this time for a purpose. There was no better time for Him to place you here. The people in this era are the people that God wanted you to impact for Him. Paul was put here at his time for the same reason. That was the perfect time for him.

Don't worry. God has thought this all through. Paul realized he was not going to get another chance at this. If he was going to do something for God, then he better do it during his life time. He saw his life as something unique. He actually did not see it as his life at all. It wasn't his life. It was his turn to make an impact for Christ. Every morning when Paul woke up, he set himself to the side, and allowed God to live through him that day. That is what he meant by dying daily. Every day he took himself out of the equation and told God that he would do anything He asked of him.

As you probably already know, a life and a turn are two totally different things. A turn is something that you take and usually put all your effort into. A life is something that belongs to you. It is something that you can spend at your own leisure. When we see our lives as "lives", we try to get as much out of them as we can. When we take on the "It's my life" attitude, we do whatever we want to do with it. When we see our lives as a turn rather than a life, we have a purpose that we will strive to achieve. It is no longer about gaining the most out of life or becoming a well known name. Now we see it in a whole new perspective. It's our turn!

One day God put us on this earth and set us loose to get a certain job done. It's our turn! We get one shot at this. Will we give it all we have, or will we do whatever we want to? After all, it is our life anyway?

Try to imagine something with me. Somehow I have been chosen to play for a major league baseball team. Ok, I know, we're stretching things again. Just humor me for a second. It is the bottom of the ninth and it is the World Series. The temperature outside is hot enough to cook an egg on the sidewalk. The score is 11 to 10. My team is behind. We already have 2 outs and the coach has asked me to go out and give it all I have. Before I go out, the coach puts his hand on my shoulder and looks me straight in the eyes. With a very sincere tone in his voice, he says, "I am putting you out there, because I need you. The whole team is counting on you to give it your all." I can see that this game is extremely important to him. He has spent his whole life trying to get a team to the World Series and it has finally happened. I am standing in the middle of this man's dream come true. As I turn to walk out onto the field, he calls my name one more time. Curiously, I turn towards him and I hear him whisper, "Go get 'em. It's your turn".

With that, I run out onto the field and pick up my bat. I am ready to turn this game back around. As I look at the pitcher, the sweat begins to pour down my face. The heat is scorching. I am extremely uncomfortable. All I want to do is to get out of the heat and get something to drink. Right then, I hear the words "Strike One!" yelled from behind me. I had just let the ball go by without even trying for it. As I try to regain my focus, I see a man selling bottled water up in the stands. While I am waving at the young man, trying to get his attention, I hear that loud voice again, "Strike Two!"

Now the pressure is on. One more strike would mean I had just lost the game for the whole team. I know how much this win means to the coach, but I am really thirsty. I had just allowed two unnecessary strikes to happen. This is my last chance to turn the game around. I look behind me and I see the rest of my team. They are sitting in the dugout drinking Gatorade, while the breeze from the fan blows through their hair. That's where I want to be. I turn back towards the pitcher, knowing that if I hit the ball I will have to run the bases. That would mean that I would have to spend more time out in the heat. The quickest way for me to get out of the heat would be to let the ball go by and strike out. I think to myself, "This is miserable. I'm tired, hot and thirsty. Why should I put myself through this? I'm still young. I have plenty of other chances to win a World Series." With that thought, I let the last ball go by and the game is over.

Before you look at me and criticize my decision, remember that this was just an example. I've never been in the World Series, and based on my athletic abilities, no one would ever ask me to be. I just wanted to show you the difference between a life and a turn.

In that story, I went out with the attitude that it was my life. My comfort was more important to me than anything else. When we think like that, we tend to focus on ourselves. What we can get out of life, our comfort, our achievements, our popularity, and so many other things become first priority. After all, it's our life. Why shouldn't we live it up? That game would have gone in an entirely different direction if I had gone out with the other mindset. It would have been my turn. That would have been my focus. It would not have been about me. It would have been about the team, the fans and most of all, the coach's dream. The heat wouldn't have stopped me from getting the job done. I would have had a goal and a purpose. I would have given it all I had because I would have realized that it was my chance to make a difference. It wouldn't have been about me. It would have been about everyone — the whole team.

Well teenager — welcome to the game. Even though God wants you to enjoy your time on this earth, He did not put you here to just live your life. You are here because He needs you. You have a purpose. You're up to bat. Is it about you or can you lay yourself to the side and let His desires become your desires? What will it be — you or Him? The time you have here on earth will be spent. It is up to you to choose <u>how</u> it will be spent. That is where that free will thing comes back into play. God will not make the decision for you. This one is up to you. Is this your life, or is it your turn to make an impact for Christ? Just remember, one of these choices will require you to try to get the most out of life without Christ. But the most out of life is something you cannot have without Christ. The other will transform you into the one thing that I have been talking about throughout this entire book — "God's Nobody". Well, are you tired of feeling like you have no purpose? You do have an assignment. You do have a purpose. Your purpose is to glorify God by giving your all for Christ.

After all Christ has done for us, why do we feel like we have the right to just live our lives for ourselves? I am not trying to say that we should not enjoy our lives — we should. I am just saying that we should enjoy it while living it for Christ. We don't know if our life will be long or short, but it has been given to us. One shot; that's all we get. Use it wisely. Seek the Lord while you are young. Don't put this off any longer. Stop trying to become "Somebody". Humble yourself and step out of the equation. Allow Him to live through you. Become a "Nobody" — but not just any "Nobody", "God's Nobody". Remember, this is not your life. It's your turn to make an impact on this world for Christ. Take your turn.

Ask Yourself This

— Do I want to see my life as a life or a turn? _____

— Am I willing to make the desires of God's heart the desires of my heart? _____

— Do I truly understand that my purpose in life is to glorify God with all that I am?

_____

_____

— Will I give my all to glorify Him? _____

_____

Memorize This:

Philippians 3:13-14 "Brethren, I count not myself to have apprehended: but this one thing I do, forgetting those things which are behind, and reaching forth unto those things which are before, I press toward the mark for the prize of the high calling of God in Christ Jesus."

Have You Totally Lost It?

Are you ready to take your turn? Are you ready to become all God wants you to be? If you are, I want you to pay close attention to this chapter. God has been waiting for this moment. He has been hoping to see you come to this point in your life for quite some time. To believe that we were placed on this earth to live life to its fullest is one of the biggest mistakes we can make. As I said before, we should enjoy our lives. The problem comes when we become more focused on our lives than we are on the cause of Christ.

Would you like to know the category of people you will be associated with if you become "God's Nobody"? I truly believe that there is no greater honor than to be "God's Nobody" and I could not be more proud than to be associated with the group of people who are. What kind of people are these? Well, God tells us in 1 Peter 2:9. *"But ye are a chosen genera-tion, a royal priesthood, an holy nation, <u>a peculiar people</u>; that ye should shew forth the praises of* *him who hath called you out of darkness into his marvellous light."*

There you have it. A "God's Nobody" is considered "peculiar". If you stop and think about it for a second, you may agree. For one thing, who wants to be a "nobody" of any kind? To the common ear this sounds insane, but I believe you understand what that truly means if you have read this far in the book. To be used of God is an awesome privilege. What greater calling could there be? If you really want to answer this calling, you need to be prepared to do things a little bit different.

This is going to require some work on your part. I would like to coach you through this one. Before we go into this game, I want you to do the one thing that will assure you a victory. Give up! Oh, what a good coach I turned out to be. That little pep talk was exhilarating wasn't it? Give up? How can you win a victory by following this advice? That's just stupid. Well, it does sound peculiar. It is just the advice you need to win though.

Let me explain. During my Lego war, when I was thirteen years old, my amnesia took over me. I no longer knew who I was or what my purpose was. I didn't even know if it was okay to be a child or not. Soon after that, God revealed to me that I needed to humble myself and trust Him. I needed to tear down the pride I had in my life and yield my control over to Him. What I was doing was acknowledging the fact that my life was nothing without Him. That is when I saw my need to become a living sacrifice for Him. I took what I saw as a valuable life, and I let it go. The reason I let it go was to get a life of fulfillment. I had to give it up to get it. I followed the instruction God had given me in James 4:10. *"Humble yourselves in the sight of the Lord, and he shall lift you up."* You see, becoming "somebody" is not our job. God already knows what we are good at, and He has the perfect plan for us. All we have to do is humble ourselves to His will. He will make us into "somebody", and when He does, we will know to give Him the credit. We will not become "somebody" because of our own efforts. He's the one who lifted us up. He should get the glory. When I realized I needed Him, because I was nothing without Him, I began to turn to Him for instruction. All I wanted to do was to let Him work through me. I gave up living my life for myself. It wasn't my life anymore. I had totally lost it.

No longer was my life being lived for myself. Now, I wanted to live for Him. My goal was to apply the words in John 3:30 to my life. *"He must increase, but I must decrease."* The identity I had built for myself was not what I wanted people to see anymore. I wanted them to see Christ in me. I wanted Him to be everything.

On that day, I believe God looked down from Heaven with complete approval. I had decided that I was going to do what was right simply because it was right to do. I just wanted to do what was pleasing in His sight. My free will was going to be used for Him, and I was going to totally surrender to do His general will for my life. I was going to do what was right; simply because it was right to do. I knew then, that it was not my life. It was my turn to make an impact on this world for Christ. It was not what I did for Christ that mattered as much as what I allowed Him to do through me.

When we can see God for who He really is, we begin to understand how undeserving we are of His love for us. I believe that if someone were to save your life, you would try to thank them for the rest of your life for doing it. Well, someone has. We are the ones that should have died the death of the cross. Christ died a horrific death. He was nailed to a cross. Thorns were crushed into His head. His beard was ripped out of His face. The bones in His body came out of joint when they dropped the cross in place. He cried out in pain and the world didn't care. He was rejected and alone. The most amazing part about all of this is the fact that He was innocent. He did not deserve it. He also had the power to stop it at any time, but He didn't. Why? Why did He suffer such a horrible death? His reason shows His love. If he had not died, you would have been lost forever. We were guilty of sin. The price had to be paid, and it was our debt. He saved our souls from Hell. I will be eternally grateful for what He did for me. That is why He will continue to be first in my life. He is somebody. He is everything to me and I am proud of who I have chosen to be for Him. Will you be willing to join me and say, "I am God's Nobody"?

Go For It!

If you are ready to let it all go and let God take you for the ride of your life, then go for it. God is ready to use you. Make Him first priority. Believe me. It's worth it!

The next page lets you know a little bit about me. I would like to know a little bit about you too. If God has used this book to give you the desire to be a "Nobody" for Him – I would love to hear from you. Please write to me at <u>joshcoverett@dayouthguy.com</u>. I am looking forward to hearing from you. God believes in you and so do I. Welcome to the game!

About the Author

J osh Coverett was born in Dearborn, Michigan. He was saved at the age of four and surrendered his life to the Lord to work with teenagers at the age of fifteen. He graduated from Baptist Bible College in Springfield, Missouri with a degree in Theology and Youth Ministries.

Josh and his wife Amy have both been working with teenagers for many years and have the desire to do so for many more. He loves to speak to teenagers and has spoken for many youth events both in the United States and the United Kingdom. He is known for his humorous speaking style and unique approach to God's Word.

Josh's number one desire is to see teenagers come to the saving knowledge of Jesus Christ and grow closer to Him each day. His love for teenagers has been evident for many years and will be evident for years to come.

For Speaking Engagements
Write to:
joshcoverett@dayouthguy.com